From Your Neighbour In A Distant Land

For all who enjoy writing

Crumps Barn Studio
Crumps Barn, Syde, Cheltenham GL53 9PN
www.crumpsbarnstudio.co.uk

Copyright © Beverley Gordon 2022

The right of Beverley Gordon to be identified as the author of this work has been asserted by her in accordance with the Copyright, Designs and Patents Act 1988.

All rights reserved. No part of this publication may be reproduced, stored in a retrieval system, or transmitted in any form or by any means, electronic, mechanical, photocopying, recording or otherwise, without the prior permission of the copyright owner.

Cover design and illustrations by Lorna Gray

Printed in Gloucestershire on FSC certified paper by Severn, a carbon neutral company

ISBN 978-1-915067-09-8

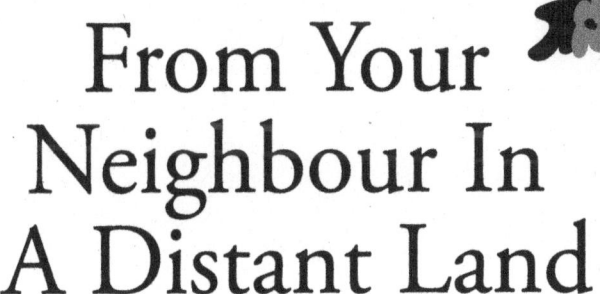

From Your Neighbour In A Distant Land

BEVERLEY GORDON

Collected Poems

Crumps Barn Studio

Dear neighbour

I promised to update you on my holiday with Nan
Well, where do I start. Nan packed for a month instead of a week
She packed all through the day and right into the night
I had only an hour's sleep, she was so noisy
Was she excited? Oh yes
For she packed for all uncertainties
If I take time to list all that she had packed
Let's just say the only thing that was missing was the microwave

I say Nan please scale back we are only going for a week
No my child all these things we will need
I say no more I want to sleep

The day arrived. I woke, rushed to the kitchen for tea
Woooow Nan did you get an invite from the Queen? You dress sooo, sooo …
Hmm, as I stopped to find the right words
Come now my child we don't want to be late.

Nan where is all your luggage?

They went on ahead

So we set off to the airport.

It took an hour. Nan talked all the way

But the driver did not mind as he just nodded and smiled

It turns out he was on the deaf side for he removed his hearing aid

As I went to give him a tip, he reached down and placed it back in his ears

And winked at me with a large grin

I wanted to burst out laughing

but then I would have to explain the joke to Nan

She would not have been impressed

Child you did not tell us we are travelling by plane

I packed for the boat

My eyes opened wide. Nan what you mean by "tell us"

She lowered her head. I packed Mr Ted

But he is dead, how can you pack him?

Oh! Ooooh!! No not dear Mr Ted

My child you know he never missed our holidays

But that was when we went camping

but now we are going far away on a plane

Why Nan why, oh why, do you want us to get arrested?
My child you have to find Mr Ted
Oh my head this is not a good start to our holiday
Not now nan we have to get on the plane

I promise I will make some calls please come now hurry
You would have thought she would be worried about her luggage
but not my nan, dearest Mr Ted is more important

This is nice as she took her seat
How fast does it drive she asked
No nan it flies.
What you mean it flies?
Look out the window, you see that long road
Well it's called a runway. The plane sets its nose towards that road
Then slowly makes its way then it builds up speed and up, up in the air it goes

Mercy me I forgot Nan never flew in a plane before
You can imagine her reaction she reached in her bag pulled out a drink

Nan where did you get that from?
As the hostess came over please fasten your seat belt
Nan was down on her knees
Madam, please you can pray in your seat the lady said
That I will certainly do but now I am looking for
the parachute

The lady was trying hard to keep a straight face
We have no parachute here
So where do you keep them?
No madam we have no such thing on the plane
I have one at home I will go and get it
Madam please that won't be necessary
We have other safety measures in place

You may wonder what I was doing at that moment
Yes sinking in my seat in dismay

The conversation continued ...

Can you open the window I need fresh air
I look at the lady please read my mind

Do not tell her the window cannot be opened
Oh shite here we go

Sorry madam this is impossible it cannot be opened
Nan eyes open wide, stood up
She raised her voice: people don't break gas
this woman said the window doesn't open

Everyone began to laugh
Madam please sit down or else I'll have to remove you
Remove me? Where?
Nan, please sit down, I will explain.
Sorry Miss, it's her first time flying
Would you like a drink, the hostess asked
Yes please
Not you, I was asking your nan
what a cheek!
No thank you dear I have one here
Madam have you been drinking? are you drunk?
Excuse me do not be impertinent, did you not just offer me a drink?
This is for medicinal purposes

Please put your seat belt on we are about to take off
So I strapped her in tight
My child I have got to spend a penny
Nan there are no shops here
She looked at me sharp. I got to wee
Not now Nan the plane is about to take off in the air
I still have time I am sure I saw a sign saying toilet up ahead
Nan come back here
Don't worry child, hold my seat

The plane took off in the air. I heard a voice say lady get back in your seat
It was too late as the plane nose head up
Nan whizzed past me on the floor as I watched in dismay
It was a sight to see
I did not know whether to laugh or cry
Horrified the lady whipped off her seat belt and rushed to her aid
With a little help she got her into a seat nearby
Once the plane had settled in the air
Nan are you alright
Yes child a little embarrassed but I will be alright

Do you still want to wee I don't know dear
Looking down at the seat oh boy!

Don't worry Nan I have you a change of clothes
Come let's get you changed
Passengers look alarmed
Come on, she is just an old lady
Less of the old, child I have many years to go
No need to hold my hand I can find my way

Please go back to your seat, safety measures will now be demonstrated
The hostess began to show us what to do in an emergency
Nan where did you get that life jacket

I have one in my handbag
I was going to put it on before getting onto the boat
Nan pulled her cord on her life jacket that turned out not to be one
Not now the lady shout aloud
Demonstration stopped the hostess ran over, the passengers were in shock
For what nan had pulled was not a life jacket

The passengers now upset demand she be removed and put somewhere else

Nan had not a care in the world

As they scrambled to dismantle the thing that Nan pulled

I'll go and get changed dear

I am so sorry I heard myself repeating

A passenger leant forward don't worry I have one

Pointing to the woman next to her fast asleep

Here take this, slip it in her drink, she will sleep all the way

Before I could open my mouth to respond to the woman I heard Nan shout

My child where does the sh**** go, does it fall on the people's heads down below

A little boy pointed that old lady said a rude word

For the preservation of love, sorry I don't want to swear

I felt my cheeks turn red

I was so tempted to take that passenger's offer

Everyone began to laugh

I don't know, come back to your seat

The hostess came back to our seat

Is everything alright would you like a tour

That may put your mind at ease

Yes please I said

once more I was not talking to you. I was getting the feeling this woman did not like me

Nan did not hesitate

The hostess took her past first class. What happened next

Well the hostess came back much later

Can you come with me please, she asked

Why? What happened? It's your Nan. My heart sank, I began to imagine the worst

Nan, Nan, I called out

Hush dear why are you shouting

To my relief there she was with a baby in her lap fast asleep

The baby in first class was crying so much in distress good old nan knew just what to do

We were then moved to first class to the relief of the other passengers

Nan looked at me and smiled. I could get use to this. What, babysitting?

No dear first class. Look real cutlery

I forgot about Mr Ted and the luggage.
That's another letter maybe
But just let say Mr Ted was not 'the' Mr Ted

What happens next I am sure you would want to know
Let me leave space in your head
For someone else's letter
It's going to be a long week with trying to find Mr Ted with my nan dearest.

Bye for now neighbour

Dear neighbours

I am here fine and well
Puzzled you must be
I wrote about me, a short story I told
On another page 'I am only human' I called it that day
I thought I was dead

Well I truly thought so but I was saved
I woke up in a nice bed even though it was not expensive cotton sheet
And a pillow smelling not so fresh but I had a bed to myself
I did not have the big breakfast but the sun did shine on my face
As I sipped my very hot cup of tea with my pinky finger in the air
There was a lady that asked of me and cried when she thought I was dead
I asked for her name, they did not say
It so happened she was passing by and heard my wild cat sounding distress
She found the cat and found me as well and called for help

Thank you I would like to say for now I have my own bed

It only temporary for I am in a hospital as you
might guess

But she left a card with her address

It said:

I heard your story from people passing by. Was it faith
that drew me to that side? For my car had broken down –
I had to walk to get help

I heard a cat in distress

As I tried to see, the light was not great.

From a distance I saw a fox staring back at me

I was scared but the cat was in distress, I could not
ignore it

That's when I saw the cat and saw you laying on the floor

When you are well, come to this address

A job you will have a room you will get for you and
your cat

Until I see you again I will take care of your cat

As for the fox he will get a treat for that day. They both
saved you.

A friend you have now

A-M Amoroso

Thank you Lady A-M Amoroso, sure to take you up on that

If you all want to know how my story went you will have to go to another page another place

Bye for now neighbour

Dear neighbours

Do you ever have a week when you wish you had stayed in bed?
Fast asleep waiting for another week to come hoping it will be different

I have two neighbours either side of me
I feel like piggie in the middle
They always want to be better than the other

Their house is of many colours
Their garden is like a beautiful paradise
They enter the garden competition by just one extra flower
The lady on my right got first prize
That did not go down well with the lady on my left
Who took second place
So she smacked the judges in the head
Well she was now band from competing any more

She was so proud she said to her neighbour
Can't top that now can you

Silly woman was so enraged she too smacked the judges in their face

Even though she had won so now she too was banned and lost first place

This competing went on

Who baked the best bread

Who had the best car, the best hairstyle

But on this particular day, the neighbour on the right was waiting for a delivery

When it had arrived they could not get it through the front door

Neighbour on the left laughed so much she fell off her chair

This made neighbour on the right so mad that she took out the window

With a lot of push and pulls she got her delivery in

What was in the box no one knows

But of course Mrs next door wanted to know

It did not take her long to know what was in the box for that very night

She broke into the house

She was not expecting to see what she saw
Like I say it has been a hell of a week
We are all in disbelief

Talk another time neighbour
I should really get back to bed

Dear neighbour

I often see your birds fly by
I wonder "where do they go"?
But the strangest thing happened. One turned and looked at me
As I peeped behind the curtains

I quickly closed my shutters
I did not see there was a letter in my tree until
Your bird picked it up and brought it to my window

I live alone. My home is somewhat grubby
That's what some would say as they pass by
But I disagree. It's lived in I would say

Some say "don't waste your time"
We hear movement inside but no one ever comes out
Some are kind in what they say but others would cross the road and keep far away

I could hear the children say "there is a witch living inside there
And she only comes out at night" then they would throw stones and run away
My house has become overgrown. I have gained weight, not much
I live on the food that I grow in my garden
I don't use my front door. My hair has grown long

I don't want to go into my story of how I got this way
But it hurts to hear what people have to say
I will just say I did have a family but they are no more
I left your letter for a day or two next to my fireplace
I wonder, who could it be from? Why me? Perhaps it was a mistake
your bird did come back, it sat and waited on the tree, I thought it must be hungry
So I went out with some seed, it flew away
I thought even the birds do not like me

I scrunched up your letter to put in the fire
I hesitated, but then threw it in
I went to make some tea

The fire was going dim so I got down on my knees to put some wood in

There was your letter all scrunched up but never got burnt

It missed the fire so even my aim was lame

I picked it up and rested it on my table next to my tea

I went to bed could not sleep I got up look through my curtain

Your bird was there fast asleep

I went downstairs, stoked the fire

Made another cup of tea, wondering why this bird did not go away

So I opened your letter

It started "Hi neighbour, How are you? Just checking on you"

It went on to say "You are not alone you have many friends"

I thought, you don't know me, what nonsense

I put your letter down and went to get some warm milk

How do I get milk if I don't go out as you are wondering

I have a goat

I picked up your letter again and started to read

As I finished my face was wet, there were tears
It took a while to compose myself
As I passed my mirror that was covered up with a cloth,
the cloth fell to the floor
I picked it up to cover it back only to glance at myself
Wow, what a sight!

At my front door, was so many letters so high, never been open just ignored
I thought and thought some more I went back to read your letter again

I took a deep sigh went to the front door
Gathering all the letters that I had ignored
It was going to be another long night
Opening every one, I read till the break of dawn
You think your letter brought me to tears yes
but in my pile of mail there was one special mail
My child my children my family
A letter from them
I will give you a little bit of my story
My wife has fabricated lies in a letter saying my children were no more

The death certificates she did post

Broken hearted I was torn apart. What did I do? Why did this happen to me?

But it was not so, she stole my children and filled their heads with lies

They too did not know of my existence for they were told I had died

In their letter they are coming to visit me

I look at the clock I have only two days to go

Where do I start, what should I do?

As my hand touches my long beard

I shaved my beard a new life of happiness ran through me

I worked all through the night, right into the morning

Neighbours staring,

"It's a man" a little girl shouted. I smiled and said goodnight

A puzzled look on their face

Yes my neighbour. It did not bother me what anyone had to say that day

The neighbour close by baked me a cake and knocked on the door

She had once left me some before but not even the cat want that

Terrible cook

She said "I am Alice. I finally get to see the person behind that long beard"

With a twinkle in her eye

Not having none of that I thought to myself, I smile "that's nice" and closed the door

I was not being rude but I have seen that look before

But thank you neighbour for my letter

You have restored me

From a neighbour with a new look on life

Hello again my neighbour

Since my last letter
Things have drastically changed, not for the better
My home got burnt down
I managed to escape
I dragged with me the man who could not find his family
Among the rubble a little baby crying
I reached down to pick it up a hand grabbed mine
A mother with a child, she could hardly speak
"Take her please she is one year old"
I lump came to my throat, tears ran down my cheeks as her hand slip off mine

I look at the child's face covered in ashes. I wrapped her in an old blanket
It was not too dark, the burning houses gave off light
"Come let's go" I say to the man, "I cannot leave, I must find my family"
As I looked around the impossible task, with buildings burning to the ground
My heart became heavy, no one is coming to rescue us

I looked at the man determined to stay, I picked up the courage

And said, I am so sorry but I have been given this child. It's a great responsibility

I must get it to safety. I cannot go alone. The journey is too great. Don't even know where I am going. Please, I beg of you, let's get to safety

The young child tied on my back was fast asleep

So off we go, where to I did not know

Among the rubble I picked up some food, something to keep us going for a day or two

There was a river not too far. I thought we would be safe

We hid behind bushes and in the trees as the bad men passed our way

A sound I pray the child did not make

When we got to the river it still was not safe two men standing there

soon it would be daylight what to do, I could not decide

The man with me was of no use, he was full of grief

I was scared I cannot lie. I could feel my heart beating out my chest

I pulled out your letter, I could not read it so I squeezed it in my hand

I remembered a line 'take courage in all your way put your trust in" I could not recall the rest

So I prayed I opened my eyes the men were not there

Panic took over I felt a hand grab mine I think my heart just stopped

But the voice whispered "come with me"

The man I drag with me got us a boat not much to look at a little hole here and there

No questions asked, I just got in

We paddled away making sure we stayed low and close to the shore

With the child still on my back, we went a distance

The man with me did not speak he just kept rowing

As dawn broke it was getting lighter

"We must go under cover we've got to ditch the boat"

"No" he said "it's the only thing we have to get away"

Since he now could speak, I asked him about the two men

He never answered he just looked me in the eye

What's this, read my mind? I looked away

The child was awake we found a place to hide the boat

There we stayed till it was dark again

I took the child and washed its face

Whilst the man opened the tins for somethings to eat

The child stared to cry for the water was cold

The man stopped and stared "where did you get that child?"

His face was full of tears

A lady I found gave her to me then she was no more

The child looked at him I looked at both of them

He drew closer in and drop to his knees

He called to the child in a language I did not recognise

My neighbour the long of the story is this child was his baby girl

As you can see I am writing to you so I must be safe

Indeed I am or should I say, we are

Thank you
From your neighbour in another land

Dear neighbour

I have a daughter a pretty little thing
I just cannot keep up with her
She so adventurous she wants to do everything
But her one problem is that she does not think
I recall we went camping, in the dark she went to pee
I told her take the torch, did she listen to me? Nope
All I know is she squatted among some stinging nettles
Our camping was cut short
Another time it was the festive season she asked about Santa
We don't have a chimney so as I went to bed, she left the window open
For him. The next morning all the presents were gone
The milk was drunk, the cookie was eaten
There was a note saying took the presents back for you did not
Leave me my favourite cookie

Yep we was burgled
That was the end of Christmas tradition.

Now she loves to listen to Miss Day cooking show
on the radio
Miss Day said get your pen and paper
For we are going to make toad in the hole
She run into my office tripping over the cat
Grabbed her paper hat
Then ran back almost falling down the stairs
As she wrote down what she could hear. The phone rang
"Get the phone" I shouted
"Get the phone, who was on the phone"
"No one's on the phone Mum"
"But did not the phone ring"
"I think so"
"Did you answer it"?
"No Mum, you said to get the phone
So here it is."
Right now I could use many word but it's best not to.

"So did you get all your ingredients?"
"I think so"
"What will you be making"?
"Toad in the hole"

"Do you need my help, after all you have not made it before?"

"No that's ok I got this. I just need a sieve

And a plastic bag" and off she went

With a puzzled look on my face at that child of mine, I shook my head

Late evening I returned home, there was police car at my door

Panicked, I ran inside "what going on?"

Calling out to my daughter she was of age

I was confronted with disbelief

Was I burgled? No that cannot be

In the kitchen I went not know what to expect

Saw two tall policemen covered in flour. Did not look impressed

My mouth could not open I could not say a word

I paused but wanted so much to laugh. I feared they might arrest me

Finally I whispered "where is my daughter"?

They pointed. "Stuck in the chimney"

Horrified I was. "Don't just stand there do something"
I shouted.

"What would you like us to do madam, the fire brigade is on its way"

"My daughter are you alright"?

"I am fine mother, I am just stuck"

"Apparently your daughter was baking toad in a hole"

"Yes I well know" As he held up a bag of live toads

I jump back "What, what, what those doing here?"

"Maybe your daughter should explain."

"Mother, Miss Day said we were going to cook toad in the hole

I was writing down the ingredients then you said get the phone

You asked me questions about the phone so I did not hear the rest

I went to the pond and caught these toads

I followed the instructions, made the batter but the toad would not sit still

they kept jumping out of my dish

It was very hard Mother

I chased them all over the house so I called for help
The policemen slipped, the flour went up in the air,
Landed on their head
The batter stuck to their feet
One toad got away it went up our chimney"
"Are you kidding me"?
The fire brigade arrived and got my daughter out
Looking like something from a horror movie
I can assure you I was not impressed

Despite those policemen's distress
A present they left
On our doorstep
Cookery book

My neighbour a hot cup of tea and long soak
I hope I don't find a toad

You have a nice day

Dear neighbour

I have a neighbour right next door
She claims to be the neighbourhood watch woman
Who's looking out for me
But I tell you she is so nosey
She spends her time peeping behind the curtain
She never misses a thing

When I am not at home she would collect my parcel
So she has an excuse to come in
I have a delivery man that does not care
he would leave my parcel anywhere
Then she would wait for me to open it so she can see what's inside

She can tell you everything
I am polite even though it's irritating
But one day I went away on holiday
She watered my plant bed whilst I was away

But I came home in a bad mood
Not knowing, she rushed over
I did not hear what she said
I screamed at her "go away, leave me alone, mind your business"
It's a day I never forget
I went inside shut the door
Laid my head to rest

Only there was no bed in fact no furniture at all
I went running out the door
I stormed over to her house even angrier than before

Bang on the door did not wait to be invited in
"My furniture, my house has been burgled"
"Would you like a cup of tea"? she asked
"Call the police I need to use you phone"
I pushed pass her
Into the front room I picked up the phone
About to dial when I caught sight of myself in the mirror looking a mess

I dropped the phone, sat down "you sure you don't want that cup of tea?"

I shook my head as I looked around
Something did not seem right
This furniture I do know
I jump up, ran up the stairs
"What's going on? These are my things
You have burgled my house, I am getting the police"

"There, there. Now you have to calm down. I did no such thing
Have a cup of tea for this is your house"
"What! Did I bang my head or had a sunstroke"?
"I don't know dear I was not there but the house you went in was mine
I was evicted. I was trying to tell you but you were in such a rage.
"But I know my house"
"Come with me dear. Look outside
Whilst you were, away every house got painted the same"

I went and sat back "I'll have that cup of tea now.

4 sugars, if you please" How long have I been away am I in a dream

"But wait then if this is my house, how did you get in?"

"The landlord gave me the key

You had a water leak so he came and fixed it

I figure you won't mind me staying here

Since you are always nice to me."

If only she knew

For I am the one that got her evicted before I went away

I must confess I also sold her precious pet

Well it kept pooping in my flower bed

But we'll keep that to ourselves

"So what are you going to do now"?

"I don't know dear,

don't you have a family

No dear I was not blessed in that department"

We had tea and a long chat.

This woman did a lot for me over the years

But all I could see was a neighbourhood rat, always in my business

But it turns out how wrong I was
I felt bad so I ask her to stay for I had plenty of space.

Bye now neighbour. No story here

Hi dear

Just a little note since she asked me to drop this letter in the post

So here I will live for I get full breakfast and good home cook meals

rent free no bills

I have my plan.

I know she was not nice to me for my cat she sold

after he kept pooping in her flower bed.

Then she wrote that letter to get me evicted

I am your neighbourhood watch woman
Be nice to me.

Dear neighbours

I have a neighbour with the nicest family you could ever meet

I never spoke to him much but when I did it would be short

The children were kind and sweet

The wife was so posh it was at times hard to take but she too was nice

So I thought

Well on this particular day her husband arrived home late

An argument started

I cannot say what it was about

But she left in a hurry, he chased after her but she was very quick

She jumped in his car and drove way

He was always sad, I tried to say hello

But never got a reply

Sometimes I would knock and call through the letter box

and leave him a cake at his front door, many neighbours have come and gone

His garden became too overgrown

But at the back he had a goat

People would stop and stare, who lives there they would say

I kept my mouth shut I would not say

One day a letter came to me by mistake but I did not know it

Or else I would not open it

Bad news it was from the wife I closed it sealed it tight

Knocked on his door No answer so I posted it through the letter box

Since then he never came out his house

Two years passed. It was time for my holiday

But I still could not get my neighbour off my mind

I was not getting closer in finding out what happened to his children

So I took a break

I went on holiday I was having such a nice time the beach was very busy

Children playing, some building sandcastles

I close my eyes tilted my hat, I'd get a nice sun tan

But out of nowhere I heard a loud shout

I recognised that posh mouth

Jumping up, I went to shout
But then I remember the letter what it did contain
But that was not right
The kids were alive all grown up and looking well
I made sure I was not seeing things

A right little detective I became, so much for my holiday
But my time was running out, my holiday soon to end
I hired a private eye
Who got the job done
The wife had remarried
It turned out she fabricated her husband death
She is now behind bars
Please, he is not to know it was me
that united him and his children and set his mind free
For a neighbour I am, he does not need to know what I did

Have a good day.

Dear neighbour

A proud Caribbean man I am
I live for the sea and enjoy the sun
a dull day, I never had none
But you know how the story goes
New government got elected So jobs were nowhere to be found
Even the fish in the sea pack them bag and leave
So I too made a dash for a new land
One called England

It was the strangest thing to see everyone moving so quickly
Things were so different, so many beggars on the streets
I was led to believe money grows on the streets
But I look down, a penny or two I did find
This I gave to the man that seemed more hungry than me

I found a job in a pub
I could not understand them nor could they understand me

They seem to speak something call Cockney

Let me see if I can remember some of the conversation

Bear with me a little please

So the man came in rubbing his head then said "I just banged my loaf of bread"

But he was not carrying any bread. I then scratch my head

Then he said "l am Hank Marvin" I stretch out my hand to say who I am

Him give me a funny look

How was I to know him was starving

Then he went to the toilet he come back vexed.

Again he say "Have you seen that pile of Wallace and Gromit"

Looking around very confuse I shake my head one way then the other way

Ahhh Yessss, Ahhh nooo, I did not know which way to stop my head

Then he pointed to the toilet

I went to look.

That's not my job I am leaving that one for the cleaner

Vomit, vomit

A pretty little gal sitting by herself, him say to her "Are you on your Jack Jones?"

Then someone shout to him "Your trouble and strife" (wife)

He legged it through the back door shouting "Joe Baxi" (taxi)

Confusion, mi head spin like a gig on a string

But when mi come with mi chat, dem look like dem nu know that

Weh yuh ah seh, small up yuhself, weh yuh deh pon

So I get another job but I buy a dictionary so I can understand

But did it make a difference? I was in a place call Birmingham

One man say to me 'alright' I say yes man me good

But him a say hello. Then another say 'ello', mi scratch mi head and move on

Head to another place them call Oxford

But it look like this new town was not like the other ones

Kiss mi neck back what a sight catch mi eye

Down the street I stop and stare, daag in handbag

One more pass mi by, dress better than me, daag a wear
suit are you kidding me

As you can see when in shock mi language come back
even though I can speaky-spokey
Nuh English that

Mi, a proud Caribbean man, a move back to mi island
It's hard work living in England
No baddy seem to understand what languages them
suppose to be on

When mi reach back to mi island mi call mi Bredda
English man you tek long fe come
Mi tell him everything even about the woman who say to
mi
Excuse me but your accent …
What about it?
Are you from the Caribbean?
Barn and raised mi de original island man
But you are white, what is your point I ask her
She could not answer so I polity say
Nuh badda mi a beg yuh lef mi beg yuh pass

Mi Bredda him laugh

look pan dis mi say

mi show him some picture of daag in handbag, daag in suit

Look man mi think we can do a thin

Daag a wear clothes so way we no mek daag cloths yuh still have dat ugly sewing machine

We gwan mek daag clothes an sell it to dem in England

Ire man

So neighbour Even though I never mek it in England

Mi mek it in mi homeland the Caribbean

Lickkle more neighbour walk gud

Hello neighbour

Hope all is well with you on the other side of the island
I have a story to tell that got me in a pickle
You'd do well to listen. Laugh if you must
Make sure you find a safe spot

There is this old man who lives in this little village where I am from
Grumpy and unkind he is to his donkey at times
But with humans it all depends on which side of the bed he got out of
Now he has a goat and a donkey to carry his load
And off to market he goes
Each day he orders the sun to dry his clothes
When the rain comes he is fine with that
but he would order it to stop when it gets too much
When he is too busy to sweep his yard he would wait for the breeze to pass
He cannot order the breeze
He tried it before. It took off his roof top

If he could catch the goat he would take it to the market to sell the milk

he would sell the milk straight from the goat

That goat was not impressed.

So he got a donkey a sweet little thing, the children would play with it

The donkey loved that

But the old man did not. He worked the donkey so hard

Sometimes the donkey would drop

On this particular day, he had half a bag full of goods for the market

But he decided to wait for the next day so the basket would be very full

As market day arrived he loaded up the donkey's back

Poor donkey struggled to carry that load

He pulled the donkey and slapped its back

The donkey cried out, the goat heard that

The hill was too steep donkey could not go up

He stood still the man pulled and pushed but the donkey refused

A passer-by said to the man "best you carry that load yourself

if you want to reach the market on time"

So the man looked at the donkey and said

"I'll show you. You are just wasting my time"

he took the basket from the donkey's back

What a sight!

I was on the rooftop looking at everything unfold

The old man struggled to carry his load

The donkey laughed at the man rolling back with his heavy load

The man never gave up. He grabbed hold of the donkey's tail

"Get me up this hill". The donkey raised his leg and kicked him

The man sat in a pile of what was in his basket and began to cry

He said "I know I have not been treating you well. This load is heavy for me

But you are a little donkey, it must be even harder for you as well"

He got up and picked up his load.

The donkey felt pity for him gave him his rope

The man tied it on the donkey

The man carried half the load on his own back and hang on to the rope

The donkey dragged him up the hill but, lo and behold,

The goat was behind the old man pushing him up the hill

It was a sight to see, that's when I fell off the roof landing in the cement

For I was laughing so much

Then I realised I now needed help. I guess someone else had the last laugh

That my story today
Have a safe day neighbour

Ps he did learn his lesson he never worked the little donkey so hard again

In fact he bought a cart. But he still can't catch that goat.

Hi neighbour

The world is a stage, so many characters everywhere
Each day an audition is taking place
Yet we put obstacles in our way
We trip we fall still many do not learn at all
They just spend their life complaining
Not me so here is what I want to say:

It's funny how a table of unexpected events can turn

My husband can sometimes be nice, sometimes even be so mean
He has at times wondered why he has a wife
But then he came home he was extra nice, my eyebrow raised
Was it old age? Whatever the case
He would shower me with gifts

I wanted for nothing he kept me on my toes
so I would not have a clue
How easily he forgets who he is married to
But this man had two hidden secrets

His compliment was too real to be true

All the while he had another home another woman on the side
I discovered this when I found a receipt
I went to his garage, I also found a book
Title: How to Keep Your Wife While Having Another Sideline

The book tells the men how to keep their wives sweet
While having another woman on the side
If you treat your wife so sweet she would not suspect

He followed the instructions like a full-blown recipe
I did not hesitate, I confronted him. He denied it, the book was not his, so he said
I kept my cool, what was I going to do?
I went back home, I did not pack his bag but I tore the back page from his book

I confronted him again when he got home, he swore
It was not true he has eyes only for me, how sweet
I ain't no man's fool

I put my plan into action

Found out who the woman was, it was obvious she did not know

Who she was dealing with

I had the choice to be her friend and get to know her at the gym or

get a job as her housekeeper

I decided on option two housekeeper

Disguised of course

She did not live close by, an hour's drive

I was horrified, he had given her a house exactly like mine, furnished in the same way

I got to know everything about her – sounds creepy right? But that's not so

She even wore the same perfume as mine. That way I would not be suspicious when he came home

I used to say to him did you mix up the bottle again? He was always in a rush

Let me cut the story short, let's jump a little back

After we argued over the book, he went off and slammed the door

I waited two days but he never came home. I rang his phone

He answered, he said if you are going to accused me

I will come to take what belongs to me

And leave the home until you come to your senses.

Going forward now

I did not answer I put my plan in action

While I was out he came and took his clothes

He kindly left a note

It said I came back for what belongs to me.

So now l packed a suitcase, hired a van and off I went

I turn up at her door use the key that she had gave me

She was in

Alarmed she was she wanted to call the police

"Really" I say, for there I was with my family and a few kids I borrowed from a friend

Put down the phone I told her.

My husband came home and left me a note it said he had came back to take what belong to him

So I thought why not help him

So here we are and here is my certificate to prove I belong to him, we belong to him

Allowed me to introduce his kids

The woman on the side as I call her dropped in her seat in shock

I said to my family go to your room I make tea someone get her a drink

The kids ran around this mighty big house

Still somewhat confused and in shock

she said "I do not know your husband"

So I pick up the photo on her mantlepiece of him

Then I place my wedding photo next to his

She took a gulp of her drink

How do you know your way around my house?

And how did you know where I live?

Well my dear you gave it to me you showed me around.

But I've never seen you before

Your housekeeper I am

What!! No way!

Your house is my house

What you talking about? I gave her some insight on this husband of mine

He had no originality

I did not let her call my husband for he was in for a surprise

That evening he came in flowers in hand typical

the same ones he bought me. He entered the room

What's going on?

I came out of the kitchen went and greeted him as I would normally do

Is that for me taking the flowers out of his hand, how nice

He froze. "hahaha" I laughed "welcome to your worst nightmare"

Well it did not take the side woman long

She attacked him with a slap

And push him out the door and kept saying I did not know I did not know

Neighbour you want to hear a funny joke?

He wrote that book long ago, yes he was once a player

I found out for I took the back page

That's it can't tell you no more.

Your neighbour somewhere

Oh you could not buy his book in the store
Exclusive it was for the gentleman club

OK ,OK, that's not how my story ended

I cannot pretend
After my husband was slapped and pushed out the door
It was not too long before the doorbell rang
I thought he had a nerve
Round two coming through
The side chick opened the door
Then she slowly step back, and back,
What's going on she step aside two men standing there
Well you can just imagine my face
Their faces were not full of smiles, in fact they were far beyond vexed
Silent hit the room apart from my noisy temporarily one day adopted kids
"Daddy" "daddy" they stopped in their tracks

"Mummy which one is my daddy"?
Hush now stop, my eye did not move from the men's expressions
Then one speak
Brother please remove your wife and kids from my house

With my tail between my legs
Oops! I say
Oh come on neighbour how was I to know he had a twin
All the year I had known him he never once mentioned him

Oh don't laugh you think it ends there?

Seriously I cannot tell you any more.
As for the book he still claims he never wrote it

Your neighbour from another land

Dear All

As neighbours we are all at a distance but a little love goes a long way
Life has many ups and down each day is never the same
There are surprises, tears, joy, laughter in every corner
But what we choose for that day is up to us

We don't know the day ahead of the one before
So let's not waste it, a little smile, a warm hello
Can brighten up another neighbour's day

You can live so near just right next door yet so further apart
Not like the days of old that are now part of a history book
Let's just take a quick look, turn the page
A new neighbour moves in next door ah even more two doors down
They are all welcome. A big smile, a great big hello
Cup of tea, a slice of cake, even flowers in a pot for their window box

Unless they live in a flat.

New children making new friends

Husbands going down the pub being introduced to the lads

Grandma finding the local church she must buy a new hat

Mavis Ivy Margaret Iris Mable Edith some of the older generation names

Mums comes to gather in the launderette getting the washing done for the week

Friday night good old fish and chips wrapped in newspaper

A little quarrel here and there

Nothing that a good cup of tea could not fix.

Yes neighbours that's history, and each person had made that back then

Generation after generation each one have contributed, putting history together

But times are changing fast, people are pulled part

It has become me myself and I

Think. Yesterday is now history what did you write on that page?

Did you do good to a neighbour or did you make their life a living hell

If someone was to ask what you did last week what history can you tell?

We are not perfect we have Adam and Eve to thank for that, and their little friend

Whose name I won't mention but deception was found in his mouth.

A new generation have come into play, what will be written in their history book?

Do you want to take a look? No ,neither do I. For we already know how that is turning out

But it's not too late to try and turn it around for we can only

Look back in time we cannot go back in person even if you change the date

So let me once again say what will be your history story today?

Have a safe, bless, good, joyous you choose
As for me, you have a nice day.

Good evening neighbour

I was very excited to get one of your letters
I would see your birds flying by, I look in my tree.
Oh nothing for me
But this morning I saw one waiting for me
So now I am excited to tell you about my day

My car broke down I had to get to town
Taxi was nowhere to be found
Never taken a bus before
What a day what an experience never have I had such a time

One hour and a half I waited for this bus
The driver gave me a smile I gave him a ten pound note
He laughed thank you for the tip he said but I cannot accept

What was he talking about?
Do you have a pass, he asked
What for, I shouted
You need to buy a seat

What! A puzzled look on my face, what for I asked

He shook his head,

The passengers shouted, is there a problem?

Madam, the driver said

Well I never. Who is this man calling madam

Kindly take that back

Please take a seat he said

I looked around. Yak grubby and not clean, I looked for one that was

OK I pulled and pulled it would not come apart

The passengers looked in horror

The driver came up to me

What are you doing?

You said take a seat, this is the cleanest one I could find

But it won't come apart

Now he laughed then his face changed

Madam

Why do you keep calling me madam I do have a name

Have you ever travelled on a bus before?

I lower my head, no but it … as I stutter to get my words out

Please just take a seat

I am trying but as you can see it won't come up

I was still pulling and tugging at the seat

Finally, it came apart, I really was pleased

His face was not. Come with me please

Bring the seat

He took me off the bus and said put it down over there, pointing to the bus stop

That looked ugly and grey

I did what he said

Now you stay there don't move until I come back

And off he drove

I don't know how long I was sitting there, but I did count a hundred cars

Did you know if you stare at the front of a car or van it resembles the driver?

Well back to my day

The driver came back with an empty bus

Shaking his head, are you still here?

Did you not say stay here?

He picked up the seat, back he went on the bus
drove off and left me standing there

You know the stupid thing I was only two roads from my house
I came home not a care, just made myself a cup of tea

And waited for my car to be repaired
What can I say, I have no time for drama

Peace out neighbour

Dear neighbour

How many of your readers have a crazy family like mine?
As the first grandchild
I do get a hard time
I don't drink or smoke but I do get pepper in my mouth
if I swear
I go to public school, it was alright for a while
Trouble seems to get the better of me
Mum travels a lot
Dad takes care of me and my brother
softly spoken and really kind is he
Grandma lives next door. She was brought up in the army
For the crazy thing she does, I am so sure

Dad could not handle me so Grandma called my mum
The day I went back to school was the day I never forget
The teacher said class welcome our new staff
Here we go I said to my friend let's have some fun
have a laugh
Boy! was I wrong
It was my mum that entered through the door

No one has ever met her before so they did not know she was my mum

You see my mum wears many wigs, I used to think she was on a secret mission

Let me speed it up. She was in my classroom

Hello children, now who would like me to sit next to them

All hands went up except mine

Ah the shy one I sit next to instead

She sat next to me, I am not shy I said

Oh well you should have had your hand up. She looked and smiled

And whispered welcome to your dad's nightmare, Daughter

What you mean mum I whispered

You will see.

Then she said aloud pay attention now.

At lunch was my aunt dressed as a dinner lady

The caretaker was my uncle

Grandma came to pick me up with knickers on her head

I jumped the school fence

I got home in one piece

Now I see what mum meant

On sports day they would run alongside me shouting my name

Then when it came to the parents' race

Mum took first place, but her wig fell off her head

Everyone stopped running for they could not stop laughing

That is how my mum won

But she did that on purpose. She doesn't like to lose

I found in her drawer an application form, I ask her what's it for

she said when a boy takes an interest.

I spoke to my dad he said he can't help I should behave myself

For he too had the same thing happened to him.

He had a tracker in his shoes so the family know where he would be

He was only 10

Just like me Dad, did you misbehave too

No daughter I got picked on a lot so they made it stop
I remember when some boys tried to push my head down a toilet bowl
They regretted the day they did that

What happened?

When my family got to hear
They made sure it would not happen again
Right through college into university my family
was there somewhere it was a nightmare even though they meant well
When I introduced your mother to my mum
My mum, that's your Grandma
let her fill out an application form

Wow, Dad! Mum must have really loved you
She did not run

You don't suppose they have a tracker on me as well?
So I started to look in my shoe

I gave it some thought then asked them to send me to boarding school

I know they couldn't follow me there, or so I thought

I know they mean well

But I am only 10

I can't guarantee I won't misbehave myself

Yes my family is extreme

My friend said I should not complain

At least they care

What do you think neighbour?

Hello again Miss nice nice

Miss goody goody
Still writing are you? I got another one of your letters
well two in fact, but I try to ignore

My cat still hasn't caught one of your birds yet
Here's hoping.
A miserable man I am
Why are you trying to be nice to me?
My own neighbours don't even like me
I suppose they too got one of your letters
They left me a letter with kind words even baked me fresh bread
It was very nice but I did not thank them
But I ate the bread it was very delicious
Quite nicely baked, any way where was I?

You're still trying to make people be nice to each other
An impossible task

I dropped them a few of my vegetables from my garden

Not that I am their friend
But it was only polite after all, they did bake me bread

Any way that's all I want to say
You are not going to make me nicey nice

Bye

Yes, hello dear neighbour

How is your day? Did you have a good week?
Plenty of letters to keep you busy

Well onto my next adventure
Bingo – remember I said in my last letter I will give it a try?
Well so I did
The building was big and bright
Everybody was busy playing
plenty of penny cards in hand
You could see I looked out of place for I was over dressed
A big smile lit up my face
Then a voice I heard said is this your first time?
I nodded my head gave a smile I made a new friend

She showed me around and show me what to do
The game was about to start
So she could not finish telling me all the rules

The man on the platform begin to shout

I look over at him, what were those funny balls jumping out

As he caught one

Then he started to shout

1 – Kelly's eye, 5 – man alive , 46 – up to tricks

And so it went on

It was so strange but I played along

I just thought he was mad

But it became very excited

I had three numbers to go

Then I was down to one

But I was not alone

The man sitting not far from me wanted

Number 54 – clean the floor

Come on number 7 I shout

What is the name for seven, I asked my new friend

Lucky seven

I shout out come on lucky seven

My neighbour, I think I got too carried away

For one moment I was on the chair, next I was on the table

My knees bent, butt in the air
Jockey style I was off
It looked like I was riding a horse
Shouting come on lucky seven
The man thought I was mad he said do you mind
I don't want to miss my 54
I shouted to him then keep your eyes on the floor
And so I continued to shout come on lucky seven
The bingo called number 9
It was anyone's game
Next minute the Mr 54 jumped on the table next to mine
Knees bent butt in the air jockey style
and started to shout come on 54
The whole place was in an uproar

For now many have hopped on their table shouting
Out their number come on 66, come on 24
It was very exciting, then the man in charge came
And tried to get me escorted out

The people were so nice they told him to leave me alone

It was the most exciting thing that happened in this place
They said

Then I heard house
What! Where, my new friend shook me, you have won
What! A house
I could not contain my excitement I rushed up to get my prize
Wait they said we have to check, check what I said
It turned out that another place another Bingo Hall
called out the same number
Something about a link she tried to explain
but who called first it had to be decided
The suspense, my pressure rose

Then a bomb dropped
Someone else took first prize
And sadly my number took second place

The room was silent I sat back down not a sound from my mouth

My new friend said never mind that's what happens
It's bingo
Excuse me, I need to pee, there I was very sad
When I came back
Mr 54 as I called him
Came up to me handed me some cash
Looking at him he said we all took a whip round
For this day was the best day we had a good laugh
Would you like to have dinner with me
So there you have it my neighbour
My number 7

Catch you later neighbour

Hello neighbour

Found one of your letters today
If you don't mind, I'd like to get something of my chest

Met with friends, catch up on the latest
A man walked over with his bad lyrics
you should have seen the look I gave him
He smiled one gold tooth shining bright, the rest of his teeth fallen asleep
His shirt open wide showing his gorilla chest
A chain dangling inside
My only thought was this man needs a lawnmower to run over that
Hairy gorilla chest
Is this seat taken, he asked. Taken where I replied
Are you with someone he asked again
I looked him in the face, is this man for real?
Are you seeing someone, he went on
Seeing where I responded
This man is a bold face

For every question he asked I gave a dumb reply
Can I buy you a drink?

That fine I can buy mine
He did not give up
My fast friend piped up – she drinks champagne
Waiter came over
Brink a bottle of your finest he said
Four glasses and one beer

I'll be back he said he got up went towards the bathroom
I said excuse me girls as the waiter pop the cork
They had a big smile

I made my way outside
There he was talking on the phone relaxed in his rented fancy car
Telling his friends who could not stop laughing
He was just a little bruck pocket man
Who was trying to impress
I slip back inside
Kept my mouth shut we all had a laugh

Yeah!! Right
He was relaxed they all drank and drank some more
he was enjoying the champagne and boasting

The bill came he looked shocked
He raised his eyes to look at me
I made no eye contact
He got up ladies I be right back he went to the bar
But I had him in my sight
Then he was off

The waiter came over and said your brother said you will take care of the bill
The girls were in shock

What! We don't have a brother
Don't worry I got this I said and dropped the cash.

Let's go I said to the girls and went out the other door
Jump in the car get in girls wow nice car they say
It's not mine just a friend's
My friends love them a lot, but scatty they are

I am sure gorilla man is still looking for his car
The scrap yard sure got a bargain
I got my money back plus interest

Bruck pocket man taking liberty

If I did not hear what he had said
I would have left my fast friends to pay his bill
But what name he called me
Well he was not getting away with that

So please don't judge me neighbour

You have a good day

Dear neighbour

I have a young son
He never wanted to mix with anyone
Not even in school
At home he spent most of his time in his room

Sometimes I would hear him speaking
But there was no one there
An imaginary friend I feel
Whenever I enter the room he would stop speaking

He would draw pictures of birds
I thought I would get him one
A sweet little bird
But the birds he drew I've never seen around here before

I asked my son about the birds he draws
He pointed to our apple tree
I looked out the window
Nothing I see, an imaginary friend may be

He was upset for I could not see any bird
So he released the bird that I gave him

Boy!! Was I upset
So I left the room
I did not shout or scream
To me my son was hard to please

I began to think when I was growing up
When no one would believe me
For the things I would see
No camera at that time
But we have camera now

That's what I did, a camera I did place
On his window hidden in a flowerpot

You are not going to believe me but I hope you will
Your bird I see a big one that my son had drawn

In his beak was the little bird that I gave my son
That he set free

Your bird brought it back to him
My son put it back in the cage

I went and climbed the apple tree there was a letter waiting for me

All along he did not have an imaginary friend phew!!
Am I relieved
Now together we have built a large bird box
where maybe your bird can have a rest
We sat together and wrote to his grandma
And to a few friends
Pet day at school he brought his bird in.

A large hall was where all the pets were shown
Everyone stood by their pets to tell their story
Some was selected to give a special presentation
My son was picked
He told about your bird carrying his bird in its beak
They laughed for they did not believe
I have proof I say,

But my son stopped me from showing the tape
He was so brave.
Afterwards, one girl came up to him and said
I believe you
For when I was sick I used to sit by my window
Here is a picture of my favourite bird

My son smiled, a smile I have never seen before
My heart leap to my mouth a little tear came to my eye
A happy parent was I, it was the same bird
I call him claws because of his big feet she said.

This is my pappa, she introduced
Why hello!! I said in my mind
I shook his hand and said a shy hi

Oh did I not mention we moved here some time ago
All his friends he had to leave behind
It's been a while since I put pen to paper
But now we look forward to spending time together my son and I

Writing to even our neighbour

Far away

That's all I want to say

A parent far away, thank you

Well good morning neighbour

What a week I have being having
I rushed out my house to catch the bus
I thought the driver was so kind
For I waved at him to wait
He looked at me and smile,
I got near he just drove away left me behind

O! yah! the bus driver ah! I remember now
Let me recap
Two days before I was waiting for the bus, it was very cold. The queue was long
When it was my turn to get on
I start to ramble through my bag for my pass
He snapped at me "hurry up just get on I am going to be late"
Upset I was and little embarrassed
I look him in the eye and said a handsome face you have
Shame you don't have the personality to match
The drive got out his seat grabbed me from behind and put me off his bus

Learn some manners he said rude woman
Are they allowed to touch?

So that was the driver who left me

Was I upset, I let my finger do the talking

Now continuing with my week

The next day my cupboard was bare
So off I went the supermarket was not far away
Today it's going to be a good day
The cloud is clear the walk will do me good

Wow the shop was very full
Well it did not matter for no one is going to spoil my day
Why do they make the shelves so high?
I stood up on tiptoe. Nope could not reach
I jump still nothing
A tall man wearing a baseball cap passed by
my cheeky self shouted not too aloud, hey handsome
He turned. Before I could finish my sentence

Another voice shout why are you calling my
man handsome

Theodore do you know this woman?

Theodore I laughed, I could not help it. Such a posh
name

She grabbed his hand and walked way

I only wanted that tin of beans you insecure woman

He is not all that anyway, I was talking to my self

Did not realise her ears were sharp

What did you just say?

I thought they had left

So I said I only wanted a tin of beans

Let me help she said and brought the whole shelf
down on me

And walked away, her man just shook his head

I picked up a tin to throw at her head, a hand
grabbed mine

Are you OK dear?

A little old lady helped me off the floor

Thank you I am fine

Then an assistant rushed over, I left him to clean up the mess

Would you help me with my basket she asked

She was so sweet

We got to the till

The old lady could not find her purse

She was getting flustered

The people in the queue started to grumble

Leave her alone she is just an old lady

I am sure you all got one somewhere

She looked at me, less of the old my dear

I have plenty of years left in me

Don't worry I said to her, then I paid for the shopping

She smiled, thank you my child

Off she went then I realised I did not have enough

To pay for mine I put my basket down and left

As I got outside I could have sworn and sworn some more

That innocent old woman was not innocent at all

In fact she was right down mean, a con-artist

She drove past me in her mighty expensive car

wound down the window and waved at me shouted out thank you my dear

I stood there like a lemon in disbelief.

The next day

An invitation came through the post I got invited to a party

I went out to buy a dress as I came out of the dressing room admiring

myself. It was a little tight, but I liked it, it was going to be a good night

The party was swinging but the room was dark

The DJ said ladies we are going to play a game

As it's singles night

All the men are against the wall you have to pick your partner to dance

Before the light comes on you have one minute

Come on my friend said. It's just a bit of fun

Not realising she had walked off

But I might get an ugly one I responded

It was very dark

I flicked my lighter there was this face staring at me not impressed

Oh! No!! Not you

My lighter dropped out of my hand

I scramble to the floor then I heard a tear, my lovely tight dress

One size too small ripped

Just then a little light came on

I turned and looked, the guy holding up his lighter

whose face was still without a smile shaking his head

Embarrassed I tried to find my way out

Tears were in my eyes

I turned and walked way really upset

Just then the music came on everyone was dancing too much to even notice

apart from that one guy

Who I somewhat called ugly in the dark, but really he was not

As I headed outside I shouted why am I having such a bad week

Then started talking to myself listing all the things that had happened to me

Can this day get any worse, it started to rain

A voice said why don't you try to be nice
Who asked you I turned angrily
He said nothing
then he took his coat off
Tried to put it over my shoulders
No thank you I am fine
I am sure you are
He said with a warm smile
That's shut me up

So he took pity on me
You want to come back inside the party's only just getting started
You still owe this ugly guy a dance
I lowered my head in shame and say sorry
Then I left still wearing his jacket he just stood there and stared
Who was he you are wondering
Was it the man in the supermarket who I asked for help?
Or was it the bus driver

Did I see him again?

Have a good week neighbour

Dear Neighbours

It's wonderful to hear from so many of you
Your highs and your lows, some make me laugh, some make
Me cry. We all are not so different
Same story just different place
But pulling together sharing thoughts and ideas
You will find long lasting friendship and joy
You have all taken your time to tell your story and express your feelings
In a way that many can relate to
It's encouraging to others for you did not hold back
When we give thoughts to our neighbours we show an expression of love
Just putting pen to paper relieves stress, clears the head
And keeps your postman in a job
It's a small world but there is a big heart inside
Even Mr Grumpy needs a letter with love
Would you not agree Mr Grumpy?

Oh, just a reminder – look where you step
I had a letter from the Ants, they were not happy
With Mr big feet.

You all have a good day now
Your neighbour with love

A Note from the Author

Enjoy, have fun, expand your imagination
Make the world a happy place with your writing
All characters are fictional

About the Author

Beverley Gordon is the author of four poetry collections: *My Very Tree, Letters From Your Neighbour Far Away* and its sequel *From Your Neighbour In A Distant Land,* and *Love Covers All Things.*

She is a mother and grandmother, and lives and works in London.